Your World

Shopping SECRETS

Multiplication

Michelle Jovin, M.A.

Consultants

Michele Ogden, Ed.D
Principal, Irvine Unified School District

Jennifer Robertson, M.A.Ed.
Teacher, Huntington Beach City School District

Publishing Credits
Rachelle Cracchiolo, M.S.Ed., *Publisher*
Conni Medina, M.A.Ed., *Managing Editor*
Dona Herweck Rice, *Series Developer*
Emily R. Smith, M.A.Ed., *Series Developer*
Diana Kenney, M.A.Ed., NBCT, *Content Director*
Stacy Monsman, M.A., *Editor*
Kevin Panter, *Graphic Designer*

Image Credits: p. 8 Universal History Archive/UIG via Getty Images; pp. 8–9 Design Pics Inc/Alamy Stock Photo; p. 13 Internet Archive; p. 14 Sara Stathas/Alamy Stock Photo; p. 18 Brian Yarvin/Alamy Stock Photo; all other images from iStock and/or Shutterstock.

Teacher Created Materials
5301 Oceanus Drive
Huntington Beach, CA 92649-1030
http://www.tcmpub.com
ISBN 978-1-4807-5796-7
© 2018 Teacher Created Materials, Inc.
Made in China
Nordica.022017.CA21700227

Table of Contents

The Field Trip 4

Sections of the Store 6

Product Placement 16

Busy Cashiers 22

The Tour Concludes 24

Problem Solving 28

Glossary 30

Index 31

Answer Key 32

The Field Trip

Mr. Murphy's class is excited—it's field trip day! And today, students get to take a tour of the local market, Fresh Foods. As they get off the bus, they see Ms. Khan, the market's owner, waiting for them.

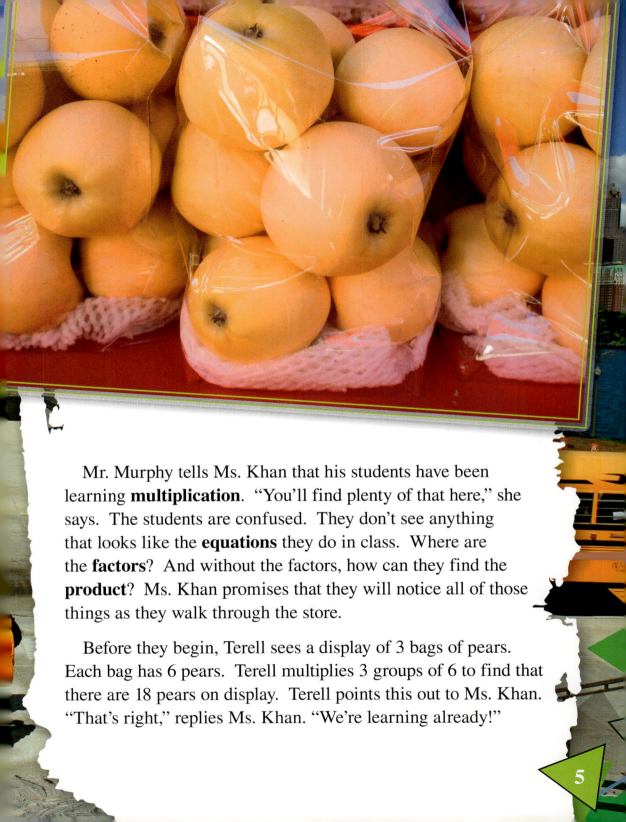

Mr. Murphy tells Ms. Khan that his students have been learning **multiplication**. "You'll find plenty of that here," she says. The students are confused. They don't see anything that looks like the **equations** they do in class. Where are the **factors**? And without the factors, how can they find the **product**? Ms. Khan promises that they will notice all of those things as they walk through the store.

Before they begin, Terell sees a display of 3 bags of pears. Each bag has 6 pears. Terell multiplies 3 groups of 6 to find that there are 18 pears on display. Terell points this out to Ms. Khan. "That's right," replies Ms. Khan. "We're learning already!"

Sections of the Store

"Now," begins Ms. Khan, "has anyone ever thought about why markets are laid out the way the are?"

"Is it so people know where to find things?" asks Victor.

"That is certainly part of the reason," says Ms. Khan. "But, market owners want to keep people inside their stores as long as possible. The longer you are here, the more likely you are to buy things. Most markets put the entrance right by the bakery, the **produce**, or the floral sections. These items look fresh and draw more people in. These areas are also very bright. That makes customers make faster decisions."

The students look around and see the bright flowers, fresh fruit, and crisp vegetables. The smell of fresh-baked bread wafts over to them. *Ms. Khan was right*, thinks Jayden. *I want to buy everything here!*

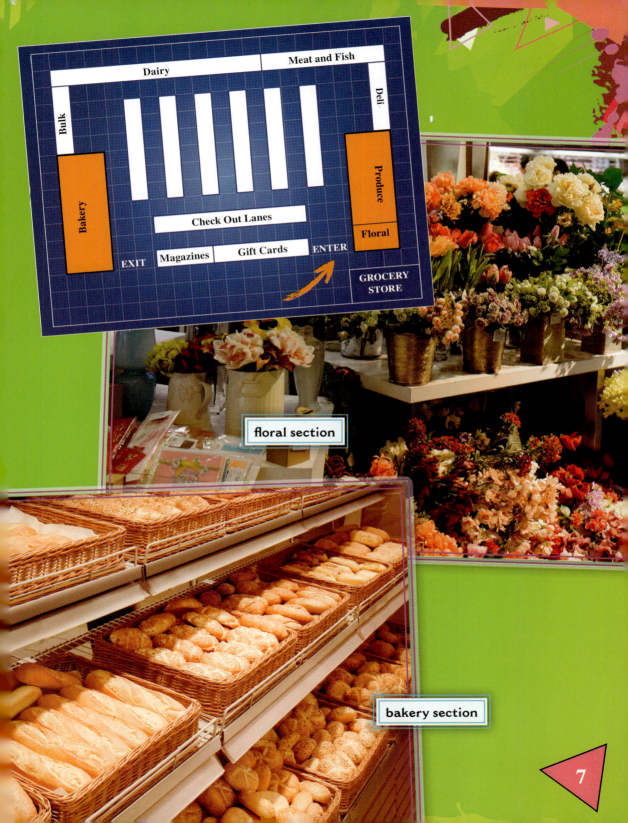

floral section

bakery section

7

The Edges

Ms. Khan begins the tour by saying that shoppers who are looking for the freshest options should stay close to the walls of the store. That is where all of the fresh produce, bread, dairy, and meat are kept. The **aisles** in the middle of the store have canned goods and other long-lasting foods.

meat market around 1900

As students walk by the deli, Ms. Khan tells them the history of markets. People used to have to go to separate stores to buy their meat, dairy, and baked goods. Markets put all of those things in one place. People liked only having to go to one store, and markets became the norm across the nation.

Ms. Khan walks over to the deli. "Who can tell me how many people are standing in line?" she asks the class.

Terell starts counting. But, Angela quickly knows the answer. She sees 2 lines with 6 people in each line. Angela multiplies 2 groups of 6 and tells Ms. Khan that there are 12 people in line. "That's right, Angela," says Mr. Murphy proudly.

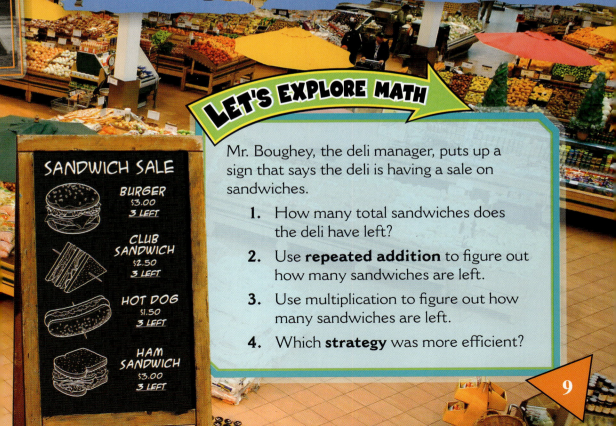

LET'S EXPLORE MATH

Mr. Boughey, the deli manager, puts up a sign that says the deli is having a sale on sandwiches.

1. How many total sandwiches does the deli have left?
2. Use **repeated addition** to figure out how many sandwiches are left.
3. Use multiplication to figure out how many sandwiches are left.
4. Which **strategy** was more efficient?

SANDWICH SALE

BURGER
$3.00
3 LEFT

CLUB SANDWICH
$2.50
3 LEFT

HOT DOG
$1.50
3 LEFT

HAM SANDWICH
$3.00
3 LEFT

Dairy Section

Ms. Khan continues walking along the inside edge of the store. The next stop on the tour is the dairy section.

Ms. Khan introduces the students to Mr. Tran. Mr. Tran is the dairy manager. "Most markets put the dairy at the back of the store for a few reasons," says Mr. Tran. "First, it's best for the dairy items to only be moved a short distance from the delivery trucks to the refrigerators. We don't want our fresh dairy to **spoil**! Plus, most shoppers will have at least one item from this section on their list. The farther shoppers have to walk through the store, the more likely they are to buy something else." Jin and Giselle look around in wonder—they had no idea so much thought went into the design of a store!

A mother and daughter browse the dairy section of a market.

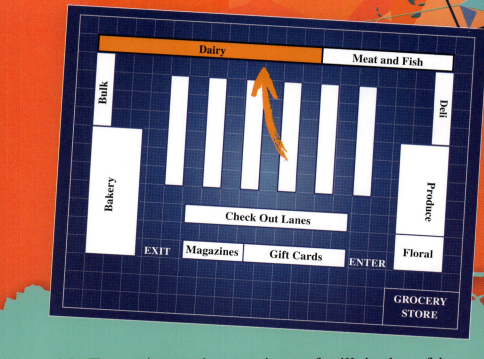

Mr. Tran points to the containers of milk in the refrigerator. "Look at the **array** of milk. Can anyone tell me how many containers of milk there are?"

Mark's hand shoots up. "Fifteen containers of milk, Mr. Tran," begins Mark. "There are three rows of five containers."

"Well done!" exclaims Mr. Tran. Mr. Murphy gives Mark a thumbs-up as they continue walking.

As Juan walks by the margarine, he sees the brand that his grandma likes to use when she bakes. Mr. Tran sees him looking and stops walking.

"Did you know that margarine wasn't always yellow?" Mr. Tran asks. "In fact, it used to be white, red, brown, black, and even pink!" The students all giggle at the thought of pink margarine.

"That's right," continues Mr. Tran. "By law, margarine had to be sold in a color other than yellow. People could dye it yellow at home. In 1950, the law changed. Margarine could finally be sold in the same yellow color as butter."

Mr. Murphy's class stares at the butter and margarine as they walk by. Juan can't help but wonder what his favorite cookies would look like if they were bright pink.

LET'S EXPLORE MATH

Mr. Tran arranges the margarine display in an array. There are 10 rows with 4 boxes each.

1. How many boxes of margarine are on display?
2. If each box of margarine is 5 centimeters tall, how tall is a stack of 10 boxes?

1947 advertisement for margarine

Aisle Style

Ms. Khan continues the tour down a center aisle, where Ms. Borne, a stock clerk, is waiting for them. "Why do some of the aisles have items at the end?" asks Kara.

"Companies pay markets to put their items in certain spots throughout the store," responds Ms. Borne. "One of those spots is at the end of an aisle. It is called an *endcap*. More people will see items on an endcap than down an aisle. So, more people might buy them."

As students walk toward the center of the aisle, Ms. Borne begins again. "We want shoppers to stay inside our store. They tend to spend more money that way. So, popular items are put in the center of aisles. That way, people have to walk to the middle of an aisle to get what they want. You might see something along the way that you want to buy." The students are amazed. So much planning has to go into the store!

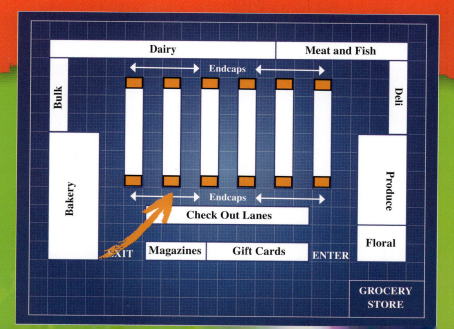

Product Placement

Ms. Borne points to a case of water on the middle shelf. "What do you notice about the items above and below this shelf?" she asks. The students look up and down.

"That case of water costs more than the water above and below it," says Nika.

"Correct!" says Ms. Borne. "Markets try to make more money by putting the most expensive items on the middle shelves. That is where most people look first. Cheaper items go above and below that. Items aimed at children will also go on the lower shelves. If kids see a bright, fun package, they might ask their parents to buy it for them."

Let's Explore Math

A case of bottled water on the bottom shelf costs $7.

1. If a case of water on the middle shelf costs 2 times as much, how much will the water on the middle shelf cost?

2. Based on the information in the previous question, how much would 3 cases of the bottom-shelf water cost? How much would 3 cases of the middle-shelf water cost?

As the tour continues, students walk past the soft drink aisle. Students notice a colorful display of root beer on the middle shelf. Mike tells Tammy that root beer is his favorite drink. "I could drink root beer at every meal for the rest of my life," says Mike.

Mr. Castro, the soft drink supplier, hears Mike and asks him if he knows where root beer comes from. "As the name suggests, root beer comes from roots. Sassafras roots, to be specific. Just boil the roots, add a few spices, and you can have root beer at home in minutes!"

"I like the sound of that!" says Mike excitedly. Mike's birthday is coming up, and he thinks about how much fun it would be to make his own root beer. *I should ask my dad to take me shopping later,* thinks Mike eagerly.

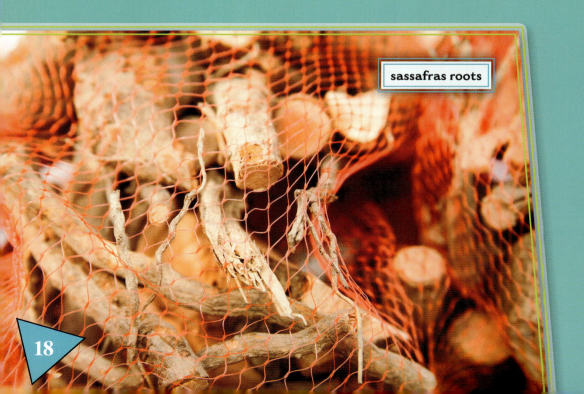

sassafras roots

LET'S EXPLORE MATH

Mike is inviting his 19 classmates to his birthday party.

1. If Mike wants his classmates to have 2 glasses of root beer each, how many glasses of root beer should he make? (Don't forget to include Mike!)

2. What if Mike decides he wants everyone to have 3 glasses of root beer instead of 2? How will this change his strategy and his solution?

While turning the corner of an aisle, Stacy sees the gift card section. This is perfect product placement! It helps her remember that Mike's birthday is coming up. *Maybe I can get a gift card*, she thinks. "How do gift cards actually work, Ms. Khan?" asks Stacy.

"I think Ms. Barr, our customer service representative, can explain it," says Ms. Khan.

"I sure can!" says Ms. Barr. "First, a customer pays the market for a gift card. The market lets the store or bank know the amount, and that card becomes **active**. Then, the customer can use the card like cash. The market takes part of the money. The rest goes to the company that provided the gift card. But, people need to actually use gift cards. Every year, more than $7 billion is spent on gift cards that don't get used! That money can end up going to the company. Some states try to return the money. But, it is difficult to find the person who bought the gift card."

Stacy thinks about her options. She sees a gift card for Sue's Soft Drink Stand. They have the best root beer in town. She is sure that Mike wouldn't let it go to waste. Stacy decides to come back to get the gift card before Mike's birthday.

LET'S EXPLORE MATH

1. How much money will Stacy spend if she buys 3 gift cards for $10 each?
2. A glass of root beer at Sue's Soft Drink Stand costs $3. How much will 4 glasses cost?
3. Will a $15 gift card be enough for Mike to drink 3 glasses of root beer? Will he have any left over? If so, how much?

Busy Cashiers

"The final stop for customers is check out lanes staffed by friendly cashiers. This is where cashiers scan items and take payments from customers," says Ms. Khan. *Math is very important in this job,* thinks Sam.

"Computers help us add the prices of the items and keep track of **inventory**," says Mr. Lund, the cashier. Students watch as Mr. Lund scans a bottle of water. The screen shows $1 added to the total. Mr. Lund then notices that the customer has 15 more bottles of water.

"What can Mr. Lund do to find the total price of all of the bottles of water?" asks Mr. Murphy.

22

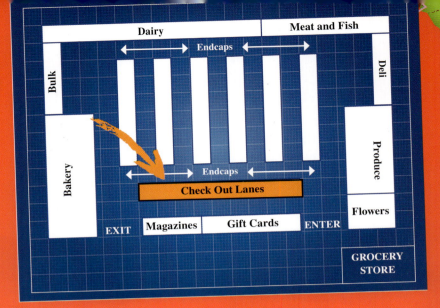

"He can scan each bottle of water as the computer adds them," says Jace.

"Yes, he could do that. Can anyone else think of a faster way?" asks Mr. Murphy.

"He can multiply $1 by 16 to find the total price," says Ann.

"That's right," says Mr. Murphy. "Both strategies will result in the same answer."

LET'S EXPLORE MATH

1. How much will 16 bottles of water cost if each bottle costs $1?
2. Jace thinks Mr. Lund should use repeated addition to find the total. Ann thinks he should use multiplication. Which strategy would you use? Why?

The Tour Concludes

"Well, students, this is the end of our tour," says Ms. Khan. The group walks toward the exit. "But first," she continues, "how about one more fun fact?" The students cheer as Ms. Khan smiles. "Does anyone know why there is only one exit from this market?"

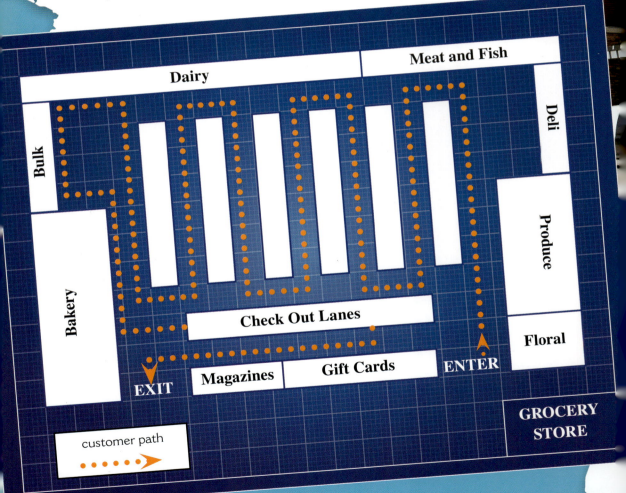

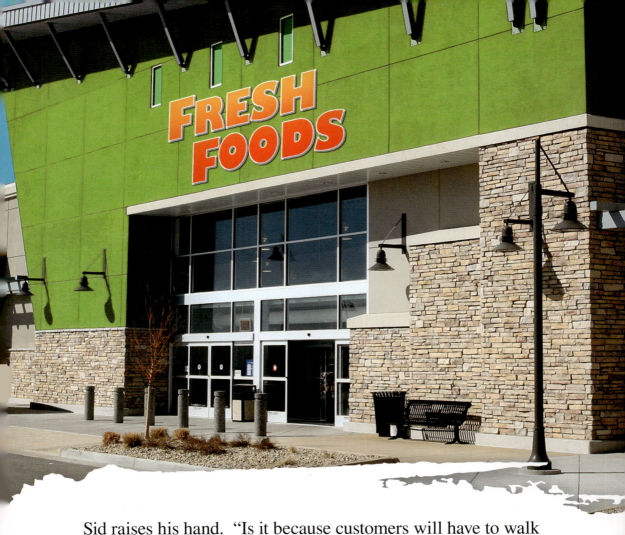

Sid raises his hand. "Is it because customers will have to walk through more of the store to get to the exit?" he asks.

"That's right!" says Ms. Khan. "With only one exit, the customer might see something along the way that they want to buy."

Sid smiles as he thinks about all that he has learned. Markets carefully plan where items should go. He never knew that so much thought goes into the layout of a store! He can't wait to tell his parents about the field trip.

The students are sad that the field trip has come to an end. But, they are excited to share what they learned back at school. And, they got to practice their math skills outside of the classroom.

Ms. Khan walks the class to the exit. "I hope you all learned a little something about how markets work. I hope you saw that math is all around you." From the arrays of milk to the cashiers scanning items, the students now see that there are many ways to multiply at the market.

As Mr. Murphy's class gets back onto the bus, they wave good-bye to Ms. Khan. Students try to stump each other with math problems on the way back to school. They think this is the best way to extend their fun day at the market.

Problem Solving

Bella and Pedro want to bake Mr. Murphy a cake to thank him for the fun field trip. They decide to talk to Ms. Khan to see what she thinks they should buy. But, when they get to the store, the baker tells them that it is Ms. Khan's day off. They have to decide what to buy on their own.

Luckily, Pedro's dad knows how to make a delicious white cake. He gives them a list of ingredients they will need to buy. Use the list to answer the questions about Bella's and Pedro's baking plan.

1. The recipe that Pedro's dad gives them will feed 10 people. What should they do to the ingredient list if they want to bake a cake that will feed 20 people?

2. Bella and Pedro also want to bake a cake for Ms. Khan. If Bella and Pedro bake 3 cakes, how many cups of flour should they buy?

3. Pedro thinks tinting the margarine pink before they bake the cake will make Ms. Khan laugh. If it takes 7 drops of pink food coloring to tint 1 cake, how many drops of pink food coloring will they need to tint 3 cakes?

2 cups sugar

3 cups margarine

4 eggs

3 cups flour

2 teaspoons vanilla extract

1 cup milk

Glossary

active—working; being in operation

aisles—spaces with shelves on both sides where people walk through stores

array—a group of objects that are arranged in equal columns and equal rows

equations—number sentences that use an equal sign

factors—numbers that you can multiply to get another number

inventory—a store's record of what items are carried and how many of each are in stock

multiplication—the act or process of multiplying numbers

produce—fresh fruits and vegetables

product—number that results from multiplying numbers

repeated addition—adding the same number again and again

spoil—to decay or lose freshness

strategy—a careful method for achieving a particular goal

Index

aisles, 8, 15, 18, 20

array, 11, 13, 27

bakery, 6

check out lanes, 22

dairy section, 8, 10

deli, 8–9

equations, 5

factors, 5

floral section, 6

margarine, 12–13, 29

multiplication, 5, 9, 23

produce section, 6, 8

repeated addition, 9, 23

Answer Key

Let's Explore Math

page 9:
1. 12 sandwiches
2. 3 + 3 + 3 + 3 = 12 sandwiches
3. 3 × 4 = 12 sandwiches
4. Possible answer: I liked multiplication better because there were fewer steps, so I found the answer quicker.

page 13:
1. 40 boxes of margarine
2. 50 centimeters per stack

page 17:
1. $14 per case
2. $21 for 3 cases of bottom-shelf water; $42 for 3 cases of middle-shelf water

page 19:
1. 40 glasses of root beer
2. Mike will have to multiply everything by 3 instead of 2. 20 guests × 3 glasses per guest = 60 glasses of root beer

page 21:
1. $30
2. $12
3. Yes, because 3 glasses cost $9, and $9 is less than $15. He will have $6 left over.

page 23:
1. $16
2. Answers will vary but may include: I think Mr. Lund should use multiplication because adding up 16 bottles of water will take longer.

Problem Solving

1. They should multiply all of the ingredients by 2 because 10 × 2 = 20.
2. 3 cups of flour per cake × 3 cakes = 9 cups of flour
3. 7 drops per cake × 3 cakes = 21 drops of pink food coloring